Written by Pamela Hickman • Illustrated by Heather Collins

STARTING WITH NATURE

Bug

BOOK

Kids Can Press

First U.S. edition 1999

Text © 1996 Pamela Hickman
Illustrations © 1996 Heather Collins

Published in Canada by
Kids Can Press Ltd.
29 Birch Avenue
Toronto, ON M4V 1E2

Published in the U.S. by
Kids Can Press Ltd.
2250 Military Road
Tonawanda, NY 14150

www.kidscanpress.com

Edited by Trudee Romanek
Series editor: Laurie Wark
Designed by Blair Kerrigan/Glyphics
Printed in Hong Kong by
Wing King Tong Company Limited

The hardcover edition of this book is smyth sewn casebound.

The paperback edition of this book is limp sewn with a
drawn-on cover.

US 99 0 9 8 7 6 5 4 3 2
US PA 99 0 9 8 7 6 5 4 3 2

Canadian Cataloguing in Publication Data

Hickman, Pamela
     Starting with nature bug book

(Starting with nature series)
Includes index.
ISBN 1-55074-475-5 (bound) ISBN 1-55074-653-7 (pbk.)

1. Insects — United States — Juvenile literature. I. Collins,
Heather. II.Series: Hickman, Pamela. Starting with nature
series.

QL474.H52 1998   j595.7'0973   C98-932151-7

Kids Can Press is a Nelvana company

Acknowledgments

Thanks to Tim, Melanie, Josh and Kelsey
for bringing me my first Luna Moth, and to
my inquisitive children, Angela, Connie and
Jenny, who are always finding new bugs to
look at.

For Ian and Andrew Forbes
PH

CONTENTS

Meet an insect   4

An insect's life   6

Insects in the water   8

Insects around you   10

Insects at night   12

Bug watching in winter   14

Hibernating insects   16

Insect migration   18

Bees and wasps   20

Giant moths   22

Insect homes   24

Insect hunters   26

Insects and you   28

Endangered insects   30

Index   32

Meet an insect

Have you seen an insect today? Maybe you saw ants on a sidewalk, a ladybug on a plant or a butterfly gliding through the air. There are twice as many insects in the world as all other kinds of animals combined. Wherever you live, you are sure to find insects nearby. They live under the ground, on the ground, in water, on plants and in the air. Some insects may even live in your home. Read on to find out more about insects and how you can get to know them better.

Insect parts

All adult insects have three body parts: a head, a middle part called a thorax, and an abdomen. A pair of antennae are attached to the head. Insects use them for touching, smelling and telling the temperature. Two large compound eyes are made up of many tiny lenses to help insects see objects and detect movement. Many insects also have simple eyes that see only darkness and light. Some insects have no wings; others have one or two pairs. Insects have no bones. Instead, they have a hard outer covering called an exoskeleton. It protects their soft body parts from being damaged.

Insect look-alikes

When you're bug watching, you'll find lots of little creatures that look like insects but are not. Earthworms, slugs, snails, centipedes, millipedes, sowbugs, spiders and daddy longlegs are some insect look-alikes. If you're not sure that what you've found is a real insect, use this checklist.

Real adult insects have: 6 legs
3 body parts
2 antennae

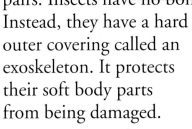

antenna

compound eye

simple eye

head

thorax

jointed leg

exoskeleton

wing

abdomen

Bugs

Although this book is about insects, we sometimes call them "bugs." People often use the word bug to mean any tiny crawling or flying animal. In science, however, true bugs are just one of many different types of insects.

An insect's life

When you were born, you were a small version of the person you are today. But most insects completely change their size, shape and color as they go through their life cycle. These changes are called metamorphosis. An adult insect may live for a few days or many years, depending on the species. Most adult insects live for a week or so, just long enough to mate and lay eggs.

Tiger Swallowtail

Complete metamorphosis

Complete metamorphosis has four stages: egg, larva, pupa and adult. Flies, beetles, butterflies, bees and ants all go through these four stages.

1. An adult insect lays her eggs.

2. A larva hatches from an egg and simply eats and grows.

3. A pupa is usually not active and doesn't eat.

4. The adult's body forms inside the pupa's skin. Then the skin splits and the adult climbs out.

Incomplete metamorphosis

Some insects, such as grasshoppers, earwigs and dragonflies, have only three stages. This type of life cycle is called incomplete metamorphosis. The stages are: egg, nymph and adult.

1. An adult insect lays her eggs.

2. Nymphs usually look like adults, except they have no wings. Nymphs eat, grow and molt until they are ready to change into adults.

3. A winged adult will search for a mate after only a few hours.

grasshopper

No metamorphosis

A few insects, such as Silverfish, hatch from their eggs as tiny versions of the adults. They simply grow larger over time until they reach adult size. As they grow, their outer skin frequently becomes too tight and they shed it, or molt, to reveal a new, larger skin underneath.

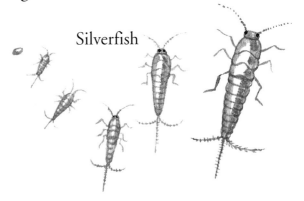

Silverfish

AMAZING INSECTS

Some cicadas spend 17 years as nymphs, buried in the ground.

An average female insect lays 100 to 200 eggs in its short lifetime, but a queen termite may lay 500 million eggs over her 50-year life span.

Insects in the water

If you go wading in a marsh, pond or river, you may see some of the incredible insects that live there. Some insects, such as water striders, live on top of the water, while mosquito larvae hang upside down, just below the surface. Diving beetles swim underwater, and dragonfly nymphs often rest on the bottom.

Aquatic insects have special ways of breathing underwater. Diving beetles and whirligigs trap an air bubble under their wing covers and use it like a scuba-diver's air tank. Mosquito larvae and rat-tailed maggots have tubelike siphons that reach above the water, like built-in snorkels. Damselfly and dragonfly larvae have gills that take oxygen directly from the water, like fish gills do.

Aquatic insects have amazing ways of moving through the water, too. The water boatman has an extra long pair of legs that it uses like oars to row itself around. A backswimmer swims on its back, which is shaped like the bottom of a sailboat. A dragonfly nymph pumps water in and out of its gills in order to breathe. By pumping the water more quickly, the nymph can propel itself forward.

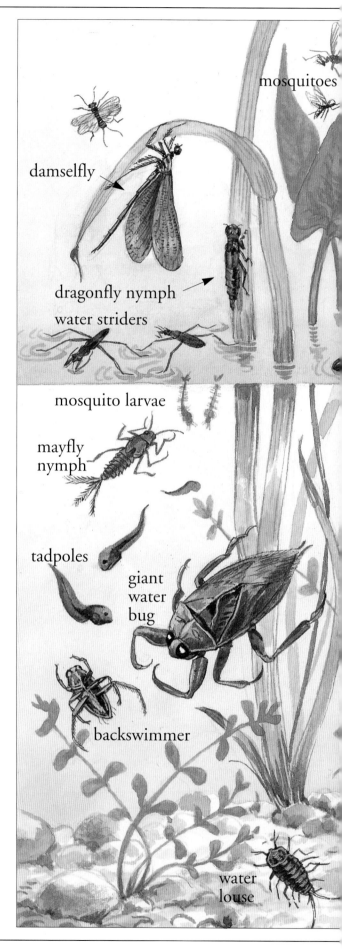

mosquitoes

damselfly

dragonfly nymph

water striders

mosquito larvae

mayfly nymph

tadpoles

giant water bug

backswimmer

water louse

whirligig beetles

water boatman

iving eetle

pond snail

freshwater shrimp

damselfly nymph

caddisfly larva

MAKE A WATERSCOPE

You can peek underwater with a waterscope and see what amazing insects live there.

You'll need:

a large empty juice can

a can opener

waterproof tape

clear plastic wrap

an elastic band

1. Ask an adult to remove both ends of the juice can and to tape the sharp edges so you won't cut yourself.

2. Spread a sheet of clear plastic wrap tightly over one end of the can. Secure it with the elastic band.

3. Tape the edges of the plastic wrap tightly to the can, all the way around.

4. Place the plastic-wrapped end of the can in the water. Be sure to keep the open end above the water. Look through the open end. How many different insects can you see in the water below?

Insects around you

One of the best ways to find insects is to go for a hike on your hands and knees. A garden trowel, a sweep net, a sheet and a magnifying glass will help you get a close-up look at the bugs around you. Look carefully, since most insects are tiny and many are well camouflaged — they are colored or shaped to blend in with their background. Remember to let the insects go back to their homes once you've looked at them.

Some beetles, ants and moth cocoons can be found under rocks or in the ground. Look for them by turning over rocks and digging in the soil with a trowel.

Use a magnifying glass to find well-hidden beetles, ants, aphids and caterpillars on tree bark and flowers.

Put a white sheet on the ground below a shrub and then shake the shrub. Bugs that are clinging to the shrub will fall onto your sheet, where you can see them.

Swing a sweep net through tall grass and flowers. Stink bugs, froghoppers, flies and grasshoppers may land in your net.

CALLING ALL INSECTS

You can get some insects to come out of hiding by offering them a sweet treat.

You'll need:

a clean soup can or plastic container

a trowel

insect bait such as honey, jam or mashed fruit

a small paintbrush (optional)

1. Dig a hole in the ground large enough to hold your container. Be sure to make the hole in a place where no one will trip in it. Place the container in the hole so the open end is even with the ground's surface.

2. Put some insect bait in the container and around the top edge.

3. After half an hour or so, check the container for insects. How many different kinds are there? After you have a close look at them, set them free.

4. Try placing your bait in different places, such as under a bush, in the woods, or in the lawn, or paint it on the trunks of different trees. Do you get different insects in each place?

5. When you are finished, remove your containers and fill in the holes.

Insects at night

You don't need to see in the dark to find insects on a summer's night. At bedtime, open your curtains and turn on the light. Soon you'll see insects flying to your window, and you may hear them landing on the screen. Look for moths, June beetles,  mosquitoes and other night fliers. You can also see nocturnal insects (ones that are active at night) gathered around porch lights and street lights after dark.

Some night-flying insects make their own light. Fireflies, sometimes called lightningbugs, are tiny beetles that light up to attract a mate. You can see fireflies in spring and early summer in fields and swampy areas.

LIGHT UP THE NIGHT

Set up a light to attract nocturnal insects and then use a magnifying glass to get a close-up look at these interesting creatures. Look for hard-winged beetles, soft, scaly-winged moths and clear-winged mosquitoes and crane flies. How do their antennae compare to each other? Using a field guide, try to identify some of the insects you see.

Banded Woollybear

June Beetle

White Underwing

Twin Spotted Sphinx

Fall Cankerworm

You'll need:

a large white sheet

an outdoor light or flashlight

some tacks

a magnifying glass

a field guide to insects

1. Using tacks, hang your sheet flat against the house under an outdoor light, or hang it from a tree and shine a bright flashlight on it.

2. When the insects land on the sheet, use a magnifying glass to see their bodies up close.

carpenter moth

Rusty Tussock

crane fly

Forester Moth

Cabbage Looper

Regal Moth

Big Poplar Sphinx

mosquito

tent caterpillar

Crocus Geometer

Garden Tiger Moth

caddisfly

Elm Spanworm

Bug watching in winter

Once you know where to go and what to look for, you'll discover that bug watching is a great year-round hobby. If you live in the south, you can find bugs any time. But if you live where the winters are cold and snowy, bug watching in winter becomes a real adventure. The colder it is, the slower the insects are. Insects are cold-blooded, which means they depend on the outside temperature to warm up their bodies and help them become active and alert. Mild days are the best times to bug watch in winter.

water striders

backswimmer

water
boatman

Check around trees or in open areas where snow is melting. If you see tiny black specks on the snow, they are probably Snow Fleas.

Ask an adult to help you find some active aquatic insects. Look for water boatmen, backswimmers and water striders in unfrozen ponds and marshes. In flowing streams you may see stonefly nymphs or adults clinging to rocks. Adult stoneflies may also be found on nearby tree trunks or the underside of bridges.

Adult Mourningcloak butterflies hibernate during the cold weather, but leave their shelter of bark or rotting logs on sunny winter days. Honeybees may also come out of their crowded hive to fly around.

House guests

If it's too cold to hunt for bugs outside, try bug watching indoors. Some insects are active all winter inside your home. You may hear a fly buzzing on the windowsill, see an ant scurry across the floor, discover a ladybug on a houseplant or find a flea on your pet.

On days when the temperature rises above 32°F, carpenter ants hibernating inside dead trees become active and begin carving out new chambers in the wood.

Hibernating insects

When you are out searching for active insects this winter, you may find some inactive ones, too. Most insects in the north hibernate to survive the cold. They stop growing, and usually don't eat or move around until warmer weather arrives. Look for different life stages of hibernating insects in shrubs and trees, in rotting logs, under rocks, in leaf litter or attached to buildings. See how many of these hibernating insects you can find this winter. Remember not to disturb the insects when you're looking at them.

Rotting logs are like apartment buildings for insects. Roll a log over or carefully peek under the bark to see if anything is hibernating there. Put the log back the way you found it.

Check twigs and plant stems for insect galls, eggs or butterfly chrysalids.

Some moth caterpillars spin their cocoons in rolled-up leaves.

In late winter, when the snow is disappearing from your garden, poke under the leaves that cover the soil. You may find some slow-moving ladybugs and other beetles that have spent the winter sheltering there.

Insect migration

You may know that many birds migrate, or fly south, for the winter, but did you know that some insects migrate too? Most butterflies form chrysalids to survive winter, but some butterflies fly south to warmer weather. In late summer and fall, masses of Monarchs leave their breeding grounds in New England and around the Great Lakes and head south to their winter home in the Sierra Madre mountains of central Mexico. There, millions of Monarchs rest in evergreen trees, sometimes called butterfly trees. In the west, Monarchs that breed in the valleys of the Rocky Mountains in Idaho and Montana return to their winter home along the coast of California between San Francisco and San Diego.

In late February, the Monarchs start to return northward. During the flight, the butterflies mate, and most of the males die. Many of the females lay their eggs on the way back and also die. The young hatch from these eggs, develop into butterflies and continue the northward trip. Some females make it all the way back from Mexico to the northern states to lay their eggs on milkweed plants there.

When the days get shorter the next fall, the new Monarchs somehow know it's time to head south.

Masses of Monarchs
Every fall thousands of Monarchs collect in the pine and eucalyptus trees on the Monterey Peninsula in California. To celebrate their arrival, children dress up like giant Monarchs for an annual parade in Pacific Grove.

Other insect migrants

Monarch butterflies aren't the only insects that fly south in the fall. Certain kinds of dragonflies, moths, beetles and short-horned grasshoppers also migrate long distances. Insects migrate for several reasons: to avoid a cold or dry season, to find food, or to find a mate.

Green Darner

short-horned grasshopper

Bees and wasps

Honeybees are known for their large hives containing thousands of bees, but most of North America's over 3300 species of bees live by themselves, make their own nests and find their own food. Most wasps are also solitary. Bees and wasps may seem the same to you, but there are some important differences.

IT STINGS!

Most bees and wasps have smooth stingers that can go in and out of a person's or animal's skin over and over again. Honeybees, however, have tiny barbs on their stingers that get stuck in the skin. When a honeybee tries to fly away after stinging only once, the lower end of its abdomen breaks off and the bee dies.

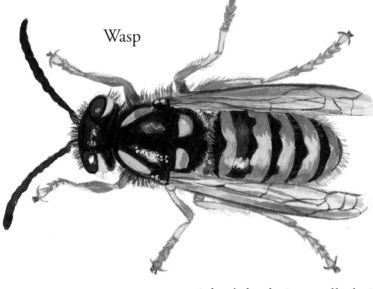

Wasp

Bee

A bee's body is usually hairier and fatter than a wasp's body.

Wasps use mud or paper for their nests. Adult wasps often sting spiders, caterpillars or other insects to feed to their young.

Bees build their nests with wax made from their bodies. Bees feed their young with plant material, such as pollen or nectar.

When you are stung, the insect injects some poison into you. To stop the swelling and itching caused by the poison, make a thick paste with baking soda and water and spread it on the sting. Some people are allergic to bee and wasp stings and must get to a doctor immediately.

Bees and wasps usually sting to defend themselves or their nests from danger. In late summer and early fall, yellow jackets start buzzing around human food and garbage. They'll sting anything that interferes with their food. You can stay safer by avoiding active bee and wasp nests (with insects buzzing around) and keeping garbage covered in warm weather.

Caution!

Have you ever noticed that road signs that mean caution or danger are often colored yellow and black? The yellow-and-black markings of bees and wasps signal danger in nature, telling other animals to stay away. Insect eaters soon learn to avoid insects with these colors because they may get stung. Harmless insects with the same coloring, such as yellow-and-black or orange-and-black caterpillars, moths and flies, are also avoided by predators. Their colors help them survive longer. This is called mimicry.

SOME BEE AND WASP LOOK-ALIKES

Clear-winged moth

Bee fly

Robber fly

Banded woollybear caterpillar

Giant moths

Cecropia Moth,
actual size

If you think all insects are tiny, you're in for a big surprise. A Cecropia Moth, America's largest, is bigger than your hand! It belongs to the family of giant silkworm moths. These moths have large, beautiful hairy bodies and long, feathery antennae. Their wings are yellowish or brownish and are decorated with eye spots. Eye spots can scare away predators, such as birds. They can also trick predators into attacking the moth's wings instead of its real head. This trick can save a moth's life.

eggs

caterpillar

From egg to adult

The eggs of giant silkworm moths hatch into tiny, spiny larvae, or caterpillars. As they grow, the caterpillars may change color several times. The full-grown caterpillars (up to 3½ in. long) are usually green or blue-green, and some have brightly colored stripes or growths on their bodies. Their favorite foods are the leaves of birch, cherry, poplar, willow and maple trees. The name "silkworm moth" comes from the many layers of silk the caterpillars spin to make their cocoons. In late summer, they wrap themselves in these silken cocoons in

Where to find giant silkworm moths, caterpillars and cocoons

Name	Range	Kinds of Trees
Cecropia	east of Rockies	ash, birch, alder, elm, maple, wild cherry, willow
Ceanothus Silkmoth	western Rockies to coast	Spicy Ceanothus, Blueblossom, Feltleaf Ceanothus
Io	east of Rockies	wild cherry, maple, birch, poplar, willow
Luna	eastern North America	hickory, walnut, Sweetgum, persimmon, birch
Promethea	east of the Great Plains	spicebush, wild cherry, Sassafras, Tulip tree, lilac

cocoon

order to survive the winter. Look for the large brown cocoons attached to twigs, or in rolled-up leaves hanging from a branch or lying on the ground. From April to June the adults emerge from their cocoons. Silkworm moths don't have any mouth parts, so they never eat and only live for about a week. They spend their short lives looking for a mate, mating and laying eggs so that more moths will be born. Adults may be found in fields, woods and backyards where the caterpillars' favorite foods grow. Look for them around lights at night.

Insect homes

The home you live in is probably made out of wood, brick or stone. Insects have homes made from wood, paper, plants, soil, mud, shells and many other materials. Here are some insect homes to watch for in your neighborhood.

paper wasp nest

If you could climb inside an anthill, you'd see many tunnels and rooms. The workers dig out the tunnels and carry the unwanted soil or sand up to the surface of the ground, making the little hill you see.

Paper wasps chew soft bark and rotting wood into a paste that they form into a nest. Look for the gray, papery nest hanging under the eaves of buildings and in other sheltered spots.

anthill

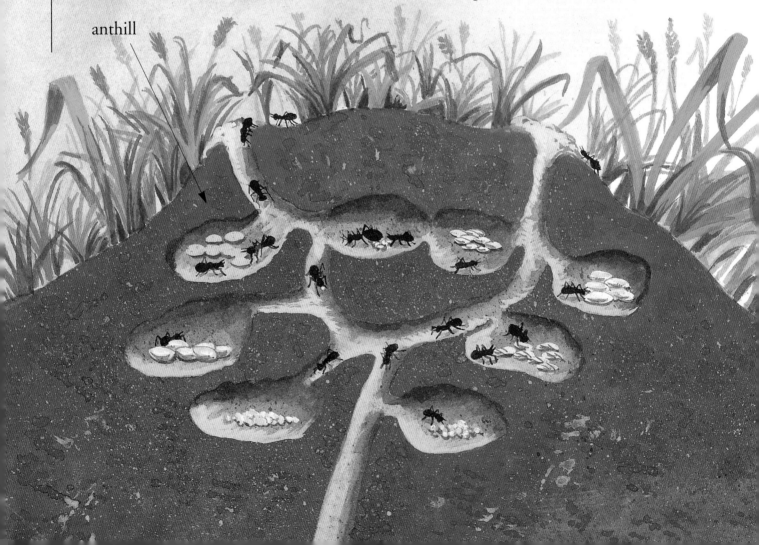

If you find a leaf with a see-through patch or path in it, then you've found a leaf miner's home. The larvae of many different kinds of insects eat their way around between the outer layers of a leaf. You can see where they have been by following the clear eating trails.

leaf miner

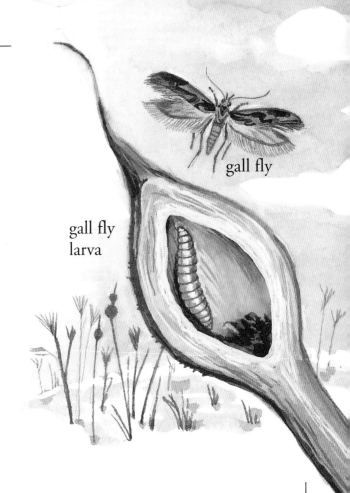

gall fly

gall fly larva

When froghopper nymphs, called spittlebugs, hatch from their eggs, they begin sucking up plant juices. They turn some of the juices into a bubbly home where the bugs hide while they develop into adults.

froghopper

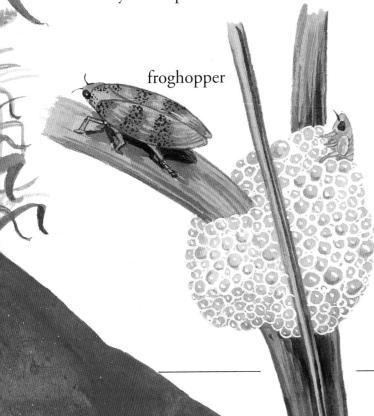

When the larva of a gall insect burrows into a plant, the plant grows around the insect and creates a gall. Inside this plant home, the larva eats all winter long, safe from the cold and hidden from predators.

Raise a gall

In the fall, look for plant galls on goldenrod stems, the tips of willow branches, oak leaves and other plants. To find out what kind of insect made the gall, keep it outside in a screen-covered jar over the winter. In late spring, bring the jar inside and watch to see what kind of adult emerges. When you've had a good look at the gall maker, let it go where you found it.

Insect hunters

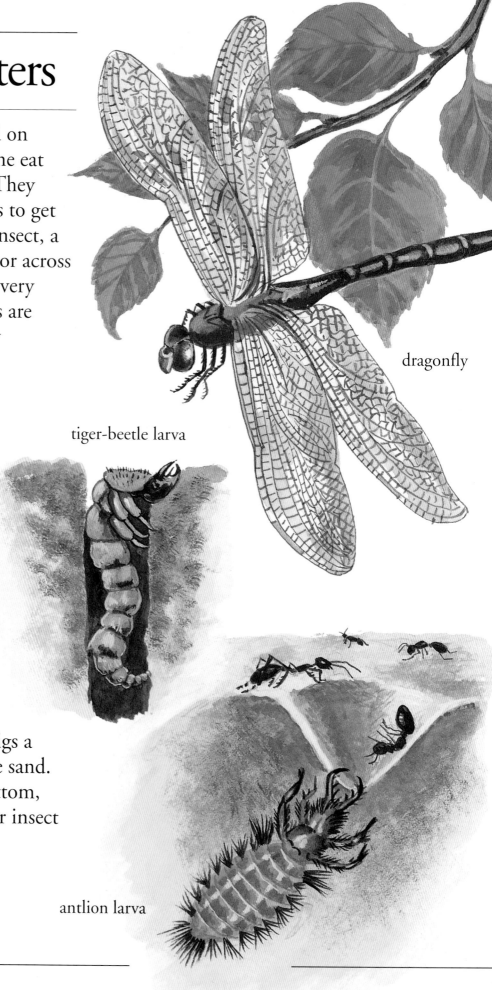

Most insects feed on plants, but some eat other insects. They have to be good hunters to get a meal. If you were an insect, a stroll through the grass or across a sandy beach could be very dangerous. These places are often full of traps set by insect hunters.

A tiger-beetle larva digs a narrow hole in the ground and then hides inside. Its large, flat head is perfectly shaped to act as a lid for the burrow. When an insect comes along, the tiger-beetle larva springs out of its hole, grabs the prey with its jaws, and pulls it into the burrow to eat it.

Antlion larvae also set traps. The antlion digs a funnel-shaped pit in the sand. Then it hides in the bottom, ready for an ant or other insect to fall into its mouth.

dragonfly

tiger-beetle larva

antlion larva

Instead of making traps, some insects have built-in equipment to help them catch their dinner. A dragonfly folds its legs together beneath its body while it is flying. This makes a trap for scooping flying insects, such as mosquitoes, out of the air. Dragonfly nymphs hunt, too. The nymph's mouth has an extra-long lower lip that is hinged on one side and unattached on the other. When prey is near, the lip quickly swings out and grabs the victim.

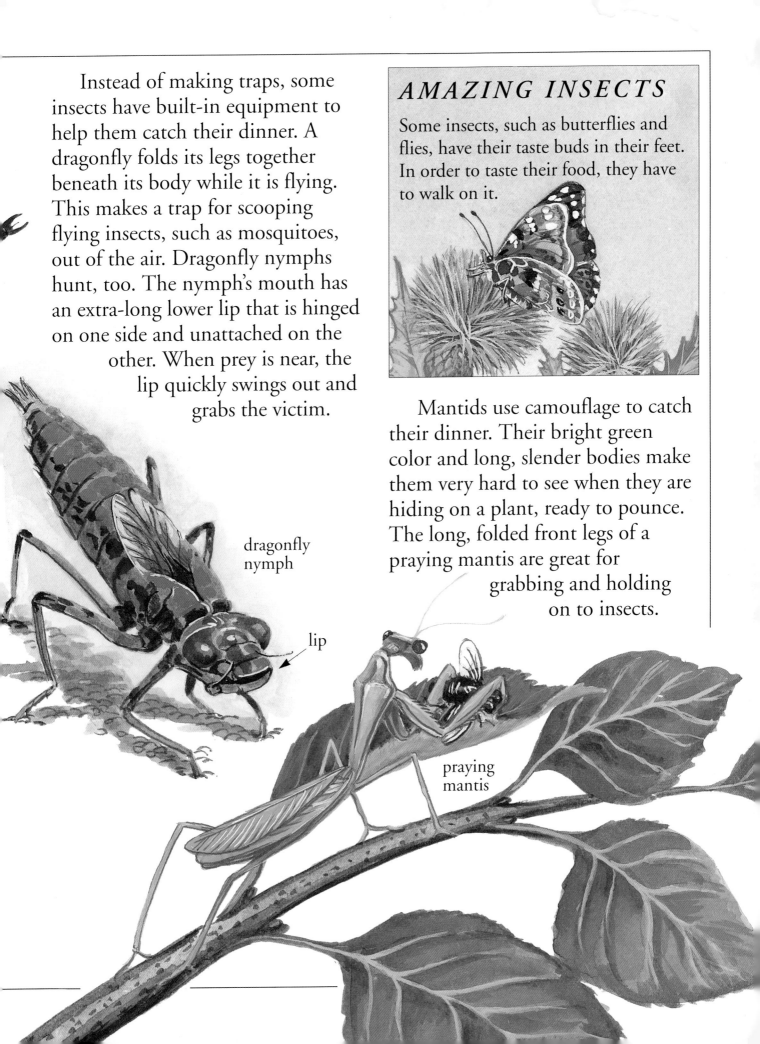

AMAZING INSECTS

Some insects, such as butterflies and flies, have their taste buds in their feet. In order to taste their food, they have to walk on it.

dragonfly nymph

lip

Mantids use camouflage to catch their dinner. Their bright green color and long, slender bodies make them very hard to see when they are hiding on a plant, ready to pounce. The long, folded front legs of a praying mantis are great for grabbing and holding on to insects.

praying mantis

Insects and you

Insects are fun to watch. They are also very important in their habitats. Many animals, such as fish, birds, frogs, turtles and bats, depend on insects as food. And plants need insects for pollination, to help them produce seeds that will grow into new plants.

People need insects too. Without insect pollinators, we couldn't grow many of the fruits and vegetables we eat. Some insects provide us with special products, such as honey, beeswax, shellac and silk. Many insects, such as fruit flies, are used in research to help us find cures for diseases. And some insects act as natural pest-controllers by eating other insects that are harmful to people or to our food crops.

AMAZING INSECTS

Honeybees need to collect nectar from 60 000 to 90 000 individual flowers to make a thimbleful of honey. Some hardworking hives make up to two pounds of honey per day.

MAKE AN INSECT FEEDER

You've heard of bird feeders. Now you can make an insect feeder. Watch how butterflies, moths, bees, flies and other nectar-loving insects drink at your feeder.

You'll need:

a new sponge about 1 in. (2.5 cm) thick

a small stone

twine

sharp scissors

a 70 oz (2 L) plastic soft-drink bottle with a lid

water

a funnel

sugar

a measuring cup

wire (optional)

1. Cut a strip of sponge 1½ in. (4 cm) wide and 6 in. (15 cm) long.

2. Ask an adult to cut a hole ¾ in. (2 cm) in diameter near the bottom on one side of your bottle.

3. Tie one end of a 8 in. (20 cm) piece of twine around the stone and the other end around the sponge.

4. Push the stone and twine and then the sponge strip into the hole in the bottle. Leave ½ to ¾ in. (1 to 2 cm) of sponge sticking out. The twine will keep the water moving up to the sponge.

5. Use the funnel to pour 1 c. (250 mL) of sugar into the bottle. Over a sink, fill the bottle three-quarters full with water, then quickly put the lid on and turn the bottle upside down. The water level should be just below the hole.

6. Carefully shake the bottle to dissolve the sugar.

7. Tie some twine or wire tightly around the bottle and hang it outside near a window, where you can watch it.

8. If you have a garden, tie your insect feeder to a post or tree trunk to attract pollinators to your flowers, fruits and vegetables.

Endangered insects

Insects need food, shelter and a place to reproduce, like all wildlife. When people drain wetlands, log forests, and plow prairie habitat, millions of insects lose their homes and die. Insects are also destroyed when we use poisons called pesticides on farms, along roadsides and in parks and backyard gardens. And collectors may threaten the populations of rare and beautiful butterflies and moths. When we kill insects, there is less food for insect-eating birds, reptiles, mammals and amphibians.

YOU CAN HELP

Here are some things you can do to help protect insects.

1. Always safely return insects to the wild after you've had a good look at them.

2. Learn to get along with insects. Everyone swats at annoying mosquitoes, but most insects are harmless, so don't hurt them.

3. Enjoy insects in the wild instead of killing them to put in a collection.

4. Put up an insect feeder (see page 28) or plant flowers in a pot or garden to give some local bees and butterflies a treat.

5. Instead of using harmful pesticides, ask at a gardening store or nursery about natural ways to control insects at your home or cottage.

6. Write to your local Fish and Wildlife Department and find out if any insects in your state are listed as endangered, threatened or rare. Ask what is being done to protect them.

7. Raise money for conservation groups that protect threatened insects and their habitats. Here are a few ideas: have a yard sale, collect sponsors for your class to clean up a local park, or put on an insect puppet show and sell tickets. Use your imagination!

Plant a butterfly banquet

You can attract butterflies by planting their favorite foods in a garden, a window box or in outdoor containers. A variety of plants, including dill, chives, parsley, carrots, lupines, cabbage, broccoli, clover and bee balm, are tasty treats for different kinds of butterflies.

Index

A
antennae, 5
aquatic insects, 8–9, 14
attracting insects, 11, 12–13,
        28–29, 31

B
bees, 20–21
    honey, 20–21
    nests, 20
    stings, 21
"bugs," 5
butterflies
    attracting, 28–29
    life cycle, 6
    migration, 18–19
    Monarch, 18–19
    taste buds, 27

C
camouflage, 10, 27
catching food, 26–27
cold-blooded, 14
collecting nectar, 28
conservation, 30–31

E
eggs, 6–7, 18
endangered insects, 30
exoskeleton, 5
eyes, 5

F
finding insects, 9, 10–11,
        14–15

G
gall insects, 25
galls, 17
giant silkworm moths, 22–23

H
habitat, 4, 10–11, 16–17
hibernating insects, 15, 16–17
honeybees. *See* bees

I
importance of insects, 28
insect eaters, 21, 26–27,
        28, 30
insect feeder, 28–29
insect homes, 24–25
insect look-alikes, 5
insect parts, 5
insect products, 28
insect stings, 21
insects and nature, 28
insects in your home, 15

L
larva, 6
life cycles, 6–7, 22–23
life span, 6–7

M
mating, 6–7, 12, 18
metamorphosis. *See* life cycles
migration, 18–19
mimicry, 21
Monarchs, 18–19
moths, 12–13, 22–23

N
night insects, 12–13
nymph, 7

P
pupa, 6

S
spiders, 5, 20
stinging insects, 20–21

W
water insects. *See* aquatic
        insects
waterscope, 9
wings, 5
winter insects, 14–15, 16–17